FROM **TREE** TO **TABLE**

by Jill Braithwaite

Lerner Publications Company / Minneapolis

Lerner Publications Company
A division of Lerner Publishing Group
241 First Avenue North
Minneapolis, MN 55401 U.S.A.

Website address: www.lernerbooks.com

Library of Congress Cataloging-in-Publication Data

Braithwaite, Jill.
    From tree to table / by Jill Braithwaite.
        p.   cm. — (Start to finish)
    Summary: Describes the process of making furniture from the planting of a tree to the construction of a table.
    ISBN: 0–8225–0947–4 (lib. bdg. : alk. paper)
    1. Tables—Juvenile literature. 2. Furniture making—Juvenile literature. [1. Tables. 2. Furniture making.]
I. Title. II. Series: Start to finish (Minneapolis, Minn.)
TS886.5.T3B73 2004
            684.1'3—dc21   2002010038

Manufactured in the United States of America
1 2 3 4 5 6 – DP – 09 08 07 06 05 04

The photographs in this book appear courtesy of:
© Todd Strand/Independent Picture Service, cover, pp. 11, 13, 15, 17, 19, 21; © Michael Rutherford/SuperStock, pp. 1 (top), 7; © Jiang Jin/SuperStock, p. 1 (bottom); © Mark E. Gibson/Visuals Unlimited, p. 3; © Inga Spence/Visuals Unlimited, p. 5; © SuperStock, p. 9; © J. Silver/SuperStock, p. 23

Table of Contents

We use tables every day.

How is a table made?

Workers plant trees.

Most tables are made from wood.
Wood comes from trees. Workers
plant trees for making tables.
The trees grow for years. They
become tall and thick.

Workers cut down the trees.

Workers use chainsaws to cut down the trees. The cut trees are called logs. Workers saw the branches off the logs.

The logs are cut into pieces.

Trucks take the logs to a **sawmill**. A sawmill is a place where logs are cut. Large saws cut the logs into long pieces called boards. Machines take the bark off the boards.

A machine makes the boards smooth.

The boards are sent to a factory where tables are made. The boards are rough. Workers put them through a machine called a **planer**. The planer makes the boards smooth and flat.

The top is made.

A worker glues some boards together to make the table's top. Tools called **clamps** hold the boards together until the glue dries. A worker uses a special machine to cut the top into the right shape.

13

The legs are made.

Most tables have four legs. A worker cuts boards to the right shape and length for the table's legs.

15

The top and legs are joined.

The legs are connected with pieces of wood called **aprons**. The aprons help support the tabletop. A worker joins the top to the legs and aprons.

The table is sanded.

A worker uses a sanding machine to make the table smooth. A clear liquid is brushed over the table. The liquid dries into a coating that protects the table from scratches and dents.

Trucks take the tables to stores.

Trucks take the new tables to stores. Stores sell many different kinds of tables. Shoppers choose the table they want, pay for it, and take it home.

200202

Pull up a chair!

A table has all kinds of uses. You can eat, read, or play a game on your new table. Pull up a chair and stay a while!

Glossary

aprons (AY-pruhnz):
pieces of wood that
connect table legs

clamps (KLAMPS): tools
used to hold things
together

planer (PLAY-nur): a tool
used to make boards
smooth

sawmill (SAW-mihl): a
place where logs are cut
into pieces

Index